W9-ASL-397

302.2   Williams, Brian.
WIL
          Communications

DATE DUE	BORROWER'S NAME	ROOM NUMBER

302.2   Williams, Brian.
WIL
          Communications

Communications

Brian Williams

Heinemann Library
Chicago, Illinois

Customer Service 888-454-2279

Visit our website at www.heinemannlibrary.com

06 05 04 03 02
10 9 8 7 6 5 4 3 2 1

Designed by Tinstar Design
Originated by Ambassador Litho
Printed in Hong Kong/China

Library of Congress Cataloging-in-Publication Data
Williams, Brian, 1959-
      Communications / Brian Williams.
         p. cm. -- (Great inventions)
      Includes bibliographical references (p.   ) and index.
      ISBN 1-58810-209-2 (lib. binding)
      1. Communication--Juvenile literature. [1. Communication.] I. Title.
II. Series.
P91.2 .W538 2001
302.2--dc21

                                              00-012381

Acknowledgments
The Publishers would like to thank the following for permission to reproduce photographs:
Corbis, pp. 4, 5, 17, 22, 26, 32, 34, 37; Erich Lessing, pp. 6, 14; AKG London, pp. 7, 12, 30; British Library, pp. 8, 13; Science Photo Library/NASA, p. 9; Mary Evans Picture Library, pp. 10, 27; Science Photo Library/Rosenfeld Images Ltd., p. 11; Culture Archive, p. 16; Science Photo Library, pp. 18 (both), 29; Science Photo Library/Ben Johnson, p. 21; Science Photo Library/Robert Isear, p. 23; Science and Society/Science Museum, pp. 24, 25, 28, 31, 38; Photodisc, p. 35; Science Photo Library/Julian Baum, p. 39; Ericsson, p. 41; Popperfoto/Reuters, p. 43.

Cover photographs: Photodisc (left and top), Ancient Art & Architecture (right)

Some words are shown in bold, **like this.** You can find out what they mean by looking in the glossary.

A note about dates: in this book, dates are followed by the letters B.C.E. (Before the Common Era) or C.E. (Common Era). This is instead of using the older abbreviations B.C. (Before Christ) and A.D. (*Anno Domini,* meaning "in the year of our Lord"). The date numbers are the same in both systems.

Contents

Introduction 4

Writing, 3500 B.C.E. 6

Maps, 2500 B.C.E. 8

Paper, 105 C.E. 10

Book, 350 12

Printing Press, 1454 14

Pencil, 1565 16

Semaphore, 1794 18

Machine-Powered Printing, 1811 20

Braille, 1829 22

Electric Telegraph, 1837 24

Postal Service, 1840 26

Fax Machine, 1843 28

Typewriter, 1868 30

Telephone, 1876 32

Fountain Pen, 1884 34

Photocopier, 1938 36

Communications Satellite, 1960 38

Mobile Phone, 1979 40

E-mail, 1982 42

Timeline 44

Glossary 46

More Books to Read 47

Index 48

Introduction

Communication means the exchange and storage of information. If you say to someone, "My name is Sarah," you are passing on information. The person you speak to needs to know the **code,** or how to understand the sounds you say—your language. That person can remember, or store, the information in his memory. You can also pass on information in other ways—by writing your name, by sending an e-mail, or even by waving flags!

How we communicate

Animals communicate in all kinds of ways. Birds sing to tell other birds that "this is my tree, keep away." A dog bares its teeth to show fear or aggression. Animals as different as bees and chimpanzees communicate using sounds and movements of their bodies.

The Rosetta Stone, bearing fragments of 2,000-year-old text in three forms of writing, solved the riddle of Egyptian **hieroglyphics.** *Found half-buried in 1799, it is now in the British Museum, London.*

However, only humans have complex languages that can be expressed in speech and written down as words and numbers. We can also use wordless forms of communication, such as when we smile, nod, wave, or shake hands. Watch when two people meet and begin talking. Notice how their hands move and how their body posture alters. This body language is part of the way people communicate with each other.

Passing on knowledge

Special communication skills make people different from animals. Since prehistoric times, humans have passed on what they had learned. At first, this was done by speech, through stories that were repeated and added to over many generations. Over the last 5,000 years, people have invented new forms of communication. The most important was writing.

Communications inventions

Inventors tried many ingenious ways to make communications easier, faster, and more accurate. Even the pencil had to be invented! Communications inventions, such as the book and the printing press, spread knowledge. Others like the typewriter and fax machine have become business aids.

In the past 150 years, there has been a revolution in communications. Ways of communicating have become so fast that they make the world seem much smaller. In 1800, it took two weeks for a letter to travel from Europe to the United States by ship. Today, we can pick up the phone to call a friend or send an e-mail any time of day. Computers store incredible amounts of information that can be sent around the world in less than a second. We can watch live television broadcasts from anywhere in the world by **satellite.**

In the 21st century, communications are changing faster than at any time in history. It's hard to predict what will happen next!

In the 21st century, mobile phones and small portable laptop computers have made instant communication possible. We can talk and send messages to practically any place in the world.

Writing, 3500 B.C.E.

Writing is a kind of organized speech—a system of marks that represent the sounds people make when they speak. Prehistoric people began to speak many thousands of years ago. Writing was invented much later, about 5,500 years ago. With writing, civilization and recorded history began.

Picture making

Before people learned to write, they drew pictures, sometimes with a stick in the sand or by daubing colored mud on a rock. More than 15,000 years ago, prehistoric people living in caves drew pictures of the animals they hunted for food.

The Sumerians wrote on tablets of soft clay using a wedge-shaped tool. The writers, called scribes, had to memorize more than 500 different signs.

The first writing

A great change happened about 10,000 years ago. Groups of people in Southwest Asia, Egypt, and China gave up hunting and became farmers. They settled in villages that grew into towns. Farmers traded food and things they made, such as clay pots, with their neighbors. They needed a system to keep records of things. How many goats did a particular person have last year? How many goats did he give to someone else in exchange for sacks of grain?

The inventors of writing—several people in more than one place—realized that pictures alone could not communicate enough information. The Sumerians, who lived in what is now Iraq, used numbers for counting. In about 3500 B.C.E., they invented other **signs** that stood for sounds, groups of sounds, or words. For example, a picture of a cat meant "cat." But a cat picture could also stand for the sound "cat," so it could be used in other words like "catch." Picture-signs became sound-signs, or what we now call letters.

Sumerian writing

The Sumerians wrote on small tablets of soft clay. They used pointed reeds or sticks to make marks, some round and others wedge-shaped. The shapes give this writing its name: *cuneiform* (wedge-shaped).

What did these first writers write about? Mostly it was business. They listed the numbers of animals on their farms and the sacks of wheat in their storerooms. When the moist clay dried in the sun, it hardened, so the lists could be kept safe for years. Some of these ancient clay writings still exist, even 5,000 years later.

Alphabets

About 3000 B.C.E., the Egyptians developed a form of writing called **hieroglyphics.** They wrote 24 signs that stood for letters or single-letter words. It was a kind of alphabet.

By about 4,000 years ago, there were several alphabets. The one we use, with 26 letters standing for different sounds, is based on that of the Greeks, who probably copied theirs from the Phoenicians. The name alphabet comes from the Greek words for A (alpha) and B (beta). Writing was used to record all kinds of information—laws, taxes, trade, religion, science, history, family letters, plays, and poetry.

People write their names as personal signs, or signatures. This is the signature of the German composer Johann Sebastian Bach (1685–1750), along with his occupation.

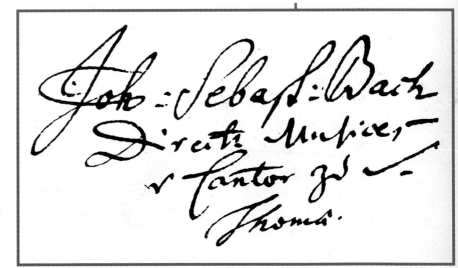

3500–3000 B.C.E.	3000 B.C.E.	Before 1400 B.C.E.	2000 B.C.E.	1000 B.C.E.	600 B.C.E.
Cuneiform writing is developed in Sumeria.	Hieroglyphic writing is developed in Egypt.	A system of Chinese characters is created.	The Phoenician alphabet is developed.	A Greek alphabet begins to be used.	A Roman alphabet begins to be used.

Maps, 2500 B.C.E.

Prehistoric hunters made long journeys, perhaps marking the way for others by making cuts in the bark of trees. They had no maps other than those in their memories, stored with familiar landmarks, such as fallen trees. They found their way by the sun and stars.

Why make maps?

We do not know who made the first map. The oldest we have found was drawn on a clay tablet about 4,500 years ago in Babylon, then a great empire in what is now Iraq. This ancient map shows villages, rivers, and mountains. The villages are the key to why the map was made. People had become farmers, living in villages, and they were trading with people in neighboring villages. A map could show the safe route from one village to the next. It could also record information, such as showing which farmers owned which fields. The local ruler used fieldmaps to record who should pay taxes on land.

Babylonians and Egyptian mapmakers

The Babylonians, who were excellent mathematicians, drew the first maps. They were the first people to divide a circle into 360 degrees, just as on a modern map Earth is divided into lines of **latitude** and **longitude.**

The Egyptians also made good maps using **geometry** to survey the land. Every year the Nile River flooded its banks and washed away farmers' boundary markers. Checking the maps settled arguments.

This world map of 1482 was based on the maps of the Greek geographer Ptolemy, who lived about 150 C.E.

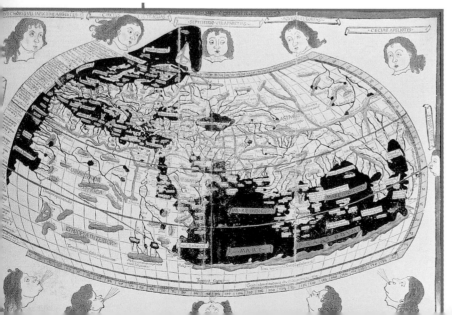

World maps

By 400 B.C.E., the ancient Greeks were sailing across the Mediterranean Sea on trading voyages. Sailors and settlers made maps of this wider world, including the Mediterranean islands, the coasts of North Africa and southern Europe, and the lands of the Middle East.

Greek geographers figured out that Earth must be round and used geometry to calculate very accurately how big it was. However, many ordinary people still believed that Earth was flat and feared sailors could fall off the edge!

Even 2,000 years later, Europeans still had nothing better than these Greek world maps. When Christopher Columbus set sail in 1492, he expected to reach Asia in a day or so. Finding the Americas in the way was a big surprise!

Each new voyage of exploration brought more information to improve maps. Using this knowledge in a new way, European mapmaker Gerardus Mercator drew the first really accurate world map in 1569. Surveyors explored the world, mapping mountains, rivers, and deserts. The science of mapmaking became more accurate in the 1920s with air photography, and in the 1960s with **satellites** in space.

Satellites began to map Earth in the 1960s. Photos taken from spacecraft gave people their first views of the entire planet.

Gerardus Mercator (1512–94)

Mercator was the greatest mapmaker of the 1500s. He was born in Flanders (now Belgium). He made globes and flat maps drawn to scale on sheets marked by grid lines. Mercator was the first to draw the round Earth accurately on a flat map. The several different ways of doing this are called projections. Distances between places on a Mercator map were roughly correct, although the shapes of continents were distorted. Mercator also produced the first atlas, or collection of maps.

2500 B.C.E.	1300 B.C.E.	1570 C.E.	1686	1855	1960s
The oldest known map is made in Babylon.	The Egyptians develop techniques for surveying land.	The first atlas, or book of maps, is produced.	The first weather map is drawn by English astronomer Sir Edmond Halley.	The first statistical maps are made, showing cholera deaths in London, England.	Space satellites transform mapmaking.

Paper, 105 C.E.

The Roman emperor Julius Caesar never wrote on paper. Many people in ancient Rome used wax tablets for sending letters to one another. After reading a wax-tablet letter, a Roman smoothed the wax and wrote an answer. It was a great way to recycle!

Papyrus

However, writing on clay or wax tablets was inconvenient. The tablet was heavy to carry and broke if you dropped it. There was another writing material, called papyrus, made from reeds. Reed stems were soaked in water and squashed in layers to make a white papery material that could be cut into sheets or rolled onto wooden rods. Papyrus reeds were also used to make mats and sandals. Only those people called scribes, whose job was to read and write, used papyrus for writing.

Parchment

Papyrus reeds grew along the Nile River in Egypt, and only the Egyptians made papyrus. Everyone else had to buy it from them. In about 200 B.C.E., the Egyptians stopped selling papyrus to the king of Pergamum in what is now Turkey. The king ordered his cleverest inventors to come up with an alternative. They produced a new writing material made from the skins of sheep, calves, and goats. Called parchment, it lasted longer than papyrus and was cheaper.

These Chinese papermakers are at work mixing plant fibers with water and then drying the pulp on screens.

How paper was invented

Paper was invented by the Chinese in about 105 C.E. The huge Chinese empire was run by thousands of officials who carried out the emperor's commands by exchanging thousands of letters written on parchment or silk. This cost too much, and the emperor told his experts to find a cheaper writing material.

An official named Ts'ai Lun came up with the answer. Maybe he had watched wasps building a paper nest. He mashed together mulberry tree bark, bamboo fibers, hemp, flax, and water until he had a soggy paste or pulp. He spread the pulp thinly over a mesh of woven bamboo and let it dry. The result was a sheet of paper. Even old fishing nets or rags could be made into paper. The cheapest paper was too coarse to write on. Chinese painters preferred smooth silk. But cheap paper was useful for wrapping and clothing.

In a modern paper mill wood pulp is the most common raw material. The dried paper flows out and is rolled onto huge reels.

The secret leaks out

For the next 500 years, the Chinese were the only people making paper. News of their invention spread only after Chinese papermakers were captured by foreigners. Papermaking reached the Middle East by 800 C.E., and by the end of the twelfth century, Europeans returning from fighting the Crusades in the Holy Land had brought the secret back with them. Soon, paper mills with water-driven machinery were hard at work pulping rags for paper. In the 1450s came an invention that needed lots of paper—the printed book.

3000 B.C.E.	150 B.C.E.	105 C.E.	1100s	1860s	1940s
Papyrus is used in Egypt.	Longer-lasting parchment starts to replace papyrus.	The first paper is made in China.	The process of papermaking reaches Europe.	The first paper bags are made.	Recycling of waste paper begins. Recycling becomes widespread in the 1970s.

Book, 350

The first books were not at all like modern paperbacks. To begin with, they were not printed. In ancient Rome, for example, all books were written by hand, usually on long strips of parchment or papyrus rolled onto wooden rods. To read this kind of book, you unwound the roll, called a **scroll.**

This engraving from the nineteenth century shows the library at Alexandria, Egypt. In the third century B.C.E., it had over 400,000 scroll-books.

In the fourth century C.E., the Romans invented a new kind of book with pages, called a codex. This was the first book that looked like a modern book. Handwritten parchment sheets were sewn and glued together between wood and leather covers. Some books were too big to be rolled on a single scroll—the Bible, for instance. One codex could contain the whole Bible, but the result was a very big and heavy book that took many hours of skilled work to make.

Books in the Middle Ages

In the Middle Ages (from 500 to 1500 C.E.), books were so precious that they were often kept chained to desks to keep people from stealing them. Each copy was made by hand, usually by monks in monasteries. The pages were decorated with ornate letters and beautiful hand-painted pictures.

A form of printing that used inked wooden blocks was invented in China and Korea before 800 C.E.. It was slow, producing one page at a time. The earliest known printed book is a Chinese book of **Buddhist** teachings called the *Diamond Sutra,* made in 868 C.E.

Most early books, such as the Bible, were either religious or historical. In Europe before 1500, most books were written in Latin. One of the first books written in English was a history of England, called the *Anglo-Saxon Chronicle.* It was begun in the ninth century.

Who read books?

Before about 1500, few people ever learned to read and write, so not many people owned books. The printing press, invented in 1454, made books cheaper, but even printed books were bound by hand—sometimes after you bought the book! After 1500, more people went to school or learned to read at home. These new readers wanted handy-sized books about everyday subjects such as poetry, cooking, and medicine, as well as big Bibles and other religious books. Publishing companies began to pay authors and sell books. After 1820, steam printing machines began turning out cheap books in cloth and paper covers by the millions.

Slice before reading

As late as 1900, books were often sold with the folded edges of pages uncut. The reader sliced the folds open with a knife to turn the pages. Paperback books first appeared in the United States in 1831 but did not become popular until several decades later. However, the mass production of these books led to a decline in quality. It was not until the 1930s that they made a comeback. Today many books are published electronically, available for downloading, and never appear in bound form.

In the Middle Ages, books were so heavy they were usually read on a desk or lectern. Many were beautifully decorated, or "illuminated."

2500 B.C.E.	350 C.E.	1045	1200s	1450s	1831
The Egyptians make scroll-books.	The oldest known codex, the *Codex Sinaiticus*, is written; 390 of its more than 700 pages survive.	Chinese printer Bi Sheng invents clay type for printing.	Paper is first used for books; they are still handwritten.	The first books are printed on presses, using movable **type.**	Paperbacks first appear in the United States.

Printing Press, 1454

Copying books by hand took so long that books were very scarce. Very few people had books in their homes before 1500. Not many people went to school. Few poor people ever had the chance to learn to read, and many rich people never bothered. Knowledge stayed closed up in a few monasteries and libraries. So new ideas spread very slowly, usually in letters written by scholars.

Gutenberg's idea

The inventor who made "books for all" possible was a German named Johannes Gutenberg, who lived in the 1400s. He came up with a new method of printing. Printing from wood blocks, just as a child stamps pictures or words with a toy printing set, had been around since before 800 in China. Wood blocks were used in Europe to print playing cards, but it was a slow process.

The Chinese had invented movable **type**—individual characters made from clay that could be arranged on a metal plate. But Chinese writing uses more than 5,000 different characters, so printing was very slow. At that time, the German alphabet had only 27 characters, or letters, so it would work well with movable type.

In this early hand printing press, the letters, or type, were arranged on a tray, called a forme. The press pushed a sheet of paper down onto the inked type.

How the press worked

Gutenberg's first bright idea was to take the screw press —an ancient invention used to crush olives and grapes— and turn it into a machine that would press a sheet of paper down onto an inked block. His second idea was to make metal type in the shapes of the characters needed. Metal lasted longer than the clay type invented in China. It could also be reused.

As a boy, Gutenberg had watched workers making coins in the city mint run by his father. He used this knowledge to make metal castings of letters, using a mixture of three metals: lead, tin, and antimony. The letters could be arranged in any order to make words and set in lines on a holder that was then brushed over with ink. A whole page could be inked at a time and printed onto sheets of paper over and over again. The letters could be lifted and rearranged as required.

Right person, right time

Gutenberg was born into a Europe bursting with new ideas. It was the period historians call the **Renaissance.** People were eager for knowledge and wanted cheaper books. Paper was readily available, and painters had developed oily inks that were ideal for printing. Improved metalworking **technology** made casting type no problem. Plenty of people knew how to use screw press machines. All this meant Gutenberg's invention had a good chance of success.

The success was spectacular. Before 1450, there were probably fewer than a million books in Europe. By 1500, about nine million books had been printed. Today, the number of books is too big to count.

Johannes Gutenberg (1390?–1468)

Gutenberg was born in Mainz, Germany, in the 1390s and probably trained as a metalsmith in Strasbourg. He spent years developing his printing press, working in secret, but he was always short of money. He had to take in partners, and in 1448 he borrowed money from a lawyer named Fust. The partners quarreled, and just as Gutenberg was about to begin printing his first book (a Bible with 1,282 pages), Fust demanded his money back. Gutenberg had to hand over the business to Fust. His Bible was printed in 1455, but by then Gutenberg was ruined. He died in 1468, poor and nearly blind.

8th Century C.E.	1454–55	1476	1490	1604	1960s
Capital and lowercase letters begin to be used.	Johannes Gutenberg prints the Bible using his printing press.	William Caxton starts the first printing press in England.	The first italic type is designed by Aldus Manutius in Italy.	The first English dictionary is compiled by a schoolteacher named Robert Cawdrey.	Computerized photo-**typesetting** begins. Modern machines can set 10,000 characters a second.

Pencil, 1565

You can write with any tool that makes a mark. The ancient Romans used sticks of lead to draw lines on papyrus sheets to keep their handwriting straight when using pen and ink. Artists drew with sticks of charcoal (burned wood), crayons (wax mixed with coloring), or chalks. They also used very thin brushes. The word "pencil" comes from a Latin word meaning "little brush."

Why pencils were needed

By the 1500s, printing was developing quickly, and more people were reading books and learning to write. They wanted to write letters or notes. Pens, however, were messy. Quill pens had to be dipped into an ink bottle. Then, to avoid smudges, the writer sprinkled sand over the paper to dry the ink.

This description of a pencil is written in Latin, the language of science in the 1500s. Graphite "marking sticks" were put inside wooden holders.

Discovering graphite

What people wanted was a writing tool that did not need ink. Someone, possibly a child, must have noticed that a soft form of **carbon,** called graphite, made marks on paper. Conrad Gesner from Switzerland wrote a description of a pencil in 1565, though this does not necessarily mean he invented it. His pencil was a wooden holder containing a rod of graphite mixed with clay. Because people thought graphite was lead, the rod of a pencil came to be called a "lead."

16

Making pencils

The first pure graphite mine was in Cumberland in northern England. People began digging out graphite there in 1564. The first pencils were made by hand, but by the 1800s, machines were making them by the millions. Machines mixed the graphite and clay and squeezed out the "leads" as long threads, like toothpaste. The leads were then sandwiched in wood and cut into pencil-lengths. Adding more clay made a harder pencil. More graphite in the mixture made a softer pencil.

From the nineteenth century, demand for pencils was huge, and making pencils by machines in factories like this one became the standard.

Still in use today

Pencils were cheap and were soon in almost every home. By the late 1800s, people could buy colored pencils, pencil sharpeners, pencils with eraser tips, and mechanical pencils.

More than ten billion pencils are made every year. Everyone uses pencils, from toddlers to the elderly. Divers can use pencils under water. Even astronauts in space find them handy, because zero gravity does not affect pencil writing.

Prehistoric times	1564 C.E.	1565	1795	1850s	1895
Charcoal, or burned wood, is used for drawing.	A pure graphite mine is discovered in northwest England.	The first written description of a pencil is made by Conrad Gesner.	Nicolas-Jacques Conté of France makes an improved pencil using powdered graphite and clay.	William Monroe of the United States invents a machine that makes pencils.	The first mechanical pencil is made, with a stock of leads inside a metal barrel.

Semaphore, 1794

For thousands of years, the fastest way to send a message overland was by horse or by pigeon. The Mongol leader Genghis Khan used pigeons in the early 1200s, and relays of messengers on horseback galloped with important letters. There was no faster way to communicate until the 1790s.

Watching for signals

People can see farther than they can hear. Visual signals, such as fires, can be seen from a long way off. A chain of beacon fires, lit one after the other, could pass on an agreed signal. In 1588, beacons were used across southern England to warn of the approach of the Spanish Armada.

At sea, sailors hoisted flags to send messages in **code.** In the flag code, each colored flag stood for a letter or number. Flag signaling worked only if ships were within sight of one another. It was aided by the invention of the telescope in the late 1500s.

Semaphore towers like this one (smaller picture) were set up at intervals of 3 to 6 miles (5 to 10 kilometers).

Getting the message

In wartime, communications are vital. In 1794, Claude Chappé, a French inventor, was asked to find a better way to send government orders at high speed. France had come though a violent revolution in 1789 and was at war with most of Europe. It urgently needed new **technology.**

Chappé and his men set up windmill-like towers on hilltops up to 12 miles (20 kilometers) apart, but within telescope range. Each tower had a long bar pivoted in the center with two smaller bars, also pivoted, at either end.

To send a message, the "arms" could be moved to 49 different positions to represent letters and numbers. The observer in the next tower noted down the message, letter by letter, and then moved the arms of his "semaphore" to pass on the signal to the next tower in the chain.

Success and weaknesses

The semaphore could send a message over 500 miles (800 kilometers) in under three minutes. Its main weakness was that it worked only in daylight and in good weather. It also needed a lot of people to run it.

The French government set up more than 550 semaphore towers across France. Britain hurriedly set up a similar system on church towers and hills. However, the war in Europe crippled any chance of commercial success, disappointing its inventor. The semaphore was used until the 1840s, when the electric telegraph replaced it.

Other uses for semaphore signals

The new railroads, begun in the 1820s, took up the semaphore idea. "Moving arm" railroad signals were used throughout the twentieth century. Flag semaphore, in which a sailor uses two flags to signal, was used at sea until the invention of radio in the early 1900s. A modern version of semaphore signaling is the baton-waving of ground crews to direct airplanes moving on the ground, although they do not use the alphabet code developed by Chappé.

1200	1588	1794	1840s	1878
Genghis Khan uses homing pigeons to carry messages.	Beacon fires warn England of the Spanish Armada's approach.	Claude Chappé sets up his first semaphore stations in France.	The new electric telegraph replaces semaphore. Railroads adopt semaphore-type signals.	Heliographs, or flashing light signals, are used by armies.

Machine-Powered Printing, 1811

Printing is a mixture of old and new inventions. Leonardo da Vinci suggested a water-driven printing press in the early 1500s, not long after the first printing press had been invented. His idea worked, but wooden presses remained the usual method for the next 300 years.

Machines take over

It was not until the early part of the Industrial Revolution (about 1750–1850) that steam power speeded up printing. The iron press was invented in about 1795 in Britain. Steam-driven presses were invented in 1811 by two Germans, Friedrich Koenig and Andreas Bauer. Their cylinder machines could print 1,100 sheets in an hour.

The new printing machines were four times as fast as the machines they replaced and needed constant supplies of paper. In 1799, Louis Robert of France had invented a machine that turned a stream of wood pulp into a 50-foot-long (15-meter-long) roll of paper. But most printers still used sheets of paper.

In 1844, Richard Hoe invented a rotary press in which the **printing plate** with the **type** was fixed around a roller. This printed 8,000 sheets an hour, about eight times faster than the existing presses. In 1865, William Bullock invented a printing press fed by giant rolls of paper instead of sheets. Most modern printing machines print on a continuous piece of paper, fed from a roll at very high speed. They print both sides of the paper at the same time.

Setting the type

Typesetting was normally done by hand, using metal letters. In the 1820s, typesetting machines with keyboards were invented. They could set type four times faster than a person working by hand. In 1884, a German-born American, Ottmar Mergenthaler, invented the Linotype machine. It had a keyboard on which a complete line of type could be arranged as a piece (or "slug") of metal from movable molds or matrices of the letters. The matrices could be used again while the "line of type," properly spaced, was being printed. The Monotype machine of 1887, invented by Tolbert Lanston, cast and set individual pieces of type. Both machines greatly speeded up typesetting.

Pictures, photography, and computers

The invention of lithography, meaning "stone-writing," made it easier to print pictures. Basically, lithography is printing on a flat surface using the principle that grease and water do not mix. It was invented in 1796 by Aloys Senefelder. He made a drawing in crayon on a stone. When the stone was wetted, the greasy drawing stayed dry, and when inked, the drawing printed onto paper. Today, metal plates have replaced the stone, and the image is a photographic one on film. The inked image is not printed directly onto paper but is first "offset" onto a rubber-covered cylinder and from there onto paper or any other material.

Modern printing machines produce everything from newspapers and books to textiles and candy wrappers.

Filmsetting using photographic film instead of metal type was a 1950s invention that was based on nineteenth-century discoveries. Filmsetting revolutionized printing because it was so fast.

Computerization of printing began in the 1950s. Electronic phototypesetters are incredibly fast, producing more than 35 million characters an hour. Text and pictures can be set up into pages using a computer program and then turned into film. From this film guide, another machine then makes the metal plates from which books, magazines, newspapers, and packaging are printed.

1796	1811	1844	1865	1904	1980s
Aloys Senefelder, a Czech writer and artist, invents lithography.	Koenig and Bauer invent the first steam press.	Richard Hoe invents the rotary press.	Continuous reel printing is used for newspapers.	Offset printing is invented in the United States.	Computerized **digital** typesetting and page make-up revolutionize printing.

Braille, 1829

How can a blind person read? Before 1800, the only way was to listen to a sighted person read out loud. People who were blind found it difficult to read, study, and find work.

Reading by touch

Louis Braille was born in 1809 in France. He was blinded at the age of three, following an accident in his father's shoemaking workshop. When he was ten, Louis was sent to the school for the blind in Paris. There, children learned to read from handmade books with raised paper letters by tracing the letter shapes with their fingers. This was difficult, and few children mastered it.

A code for reading in the dark

When he was twelve, Louis met an army officer named Captain Charles Barbier, who visited the school. Barbier had an idea that he thought might interest the teachers. He had invented an alphabet **code** using raised dots. The idea was that soldiers at night could read messages in darkness, by touch. They would not need lights and so would not give away their position to the enemy.

Unfortunately, soldiers found the code hard to learn and made too many mistakes. The army said no to Barbier's idea. But as he felt the pages of the code book with his fingers, Louis Braille became excited. Why not have a dot alphabet for blind people?

Braille writing is read by touch, running the fingers over the dots. A computer can translate ordinary print into braille.

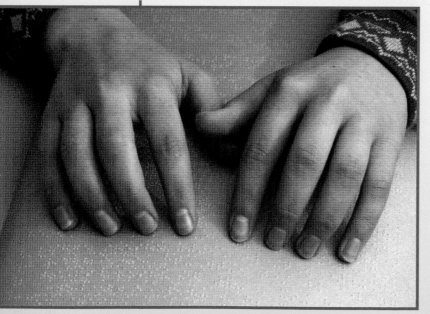

The Braille system

It took Louis Braille six years to work out a system of six raised dots with sixty-three different arrangements for letters, numbers, punctuation marks, and musical notes. He tried it out on his fellow students and found that most children learned it easily, though adults took a little longer.

In 1829, Braille published his first book with raised-dot words. It took time for his invention to catch on, but his system soon became known around the world simply as "braille." Braille is still used for reading, as well as for writing, using embossing pens or a six-key machine like a typewriter. A braille printer can even be linked to a computer.

New aids for visually impaired people

Since the 1950s, progress in electronics has provided new aids for people who are blind or have visual impairments. Many people use handy-sized tape players to play recorded books. Others use optical **scanners.** These "read" the print of a normal book and turn the text into enlarged raised letters that can be read by touch. More advanced aids "read" print in a computerized, humanlike voice.

Louis Braille (1809–1852)

Louis Braille was born near Paris, France, in 1809, and was blinded in 1812. Despite his blindness, Louis learned to read, studied science, and played the organ. He spent his life improving his reading system and teaching at his school (the Institution for Blind Youth in Paris, established in 1784), until his death in 1852.

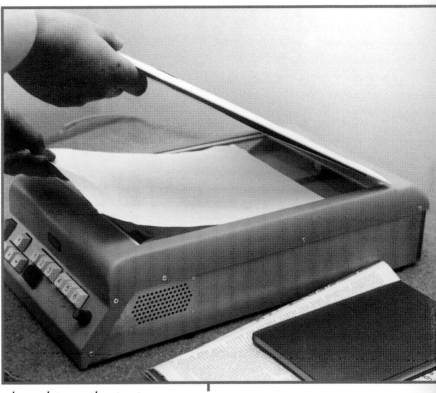

A Personal Reader uses a computerized voice to "read" letters, magazines, books, and bills. It can also store all of this information on disk.

1784	1821	1829	1955	1960s	1970s
A school for the blind is opened in Paris. It is the first in the world.	Charles Barbier shows Louis Braille his raised dot code.	The first braille book is published.	The first talking books on tape are produced.	Computerized production of braille books begins.	Optical scanners turn print into raised letters and sounds.

Electric Telegraph, 1837

Inventors experimenting with homemade "electrical machines" in the early 1800s discovered an interesting effect. An **electric current** passing through a wire could be turned on and off, and when this happened, some things attached to the wire might produce movement or noise. In 1816, British inventor Francis Ronalds showed that electric current passing through wires strung from trees in his garden could make fiber balls twitch. However, the government did not see a need for new communications systems. The country was finally at peace, after many long years of war with France.

Putting signals through wires

In 1820, Danish scientist Hans Oersted discovered that an electric current flowing through a wire would produce a **magnetic field—** a property called **electromagnetism.** In the 1830s, Michael Faraday and Joseph Henry discovered the useful reverse effect of electromagnetism. Moving a magnet near a coil of wire produced an electric current in the wire. Here was the breakthrough for a "message by wire" system. Inventors in Britain, Germany, France, Russia, and the United States raced to be first in making a telegraph, or "far-writing," machine.

The inventor of the electric telegraph, Samuel Morse, also devised a code for sending messages as dots and dashes. Morse code soon became an international "language."

The first telegraph

In 1830, Joseph Henry, working in the United States, found that several small batteries together boosted a signal better than one big battery. Two British inventors, Charles Wheatstone and William Cooke, then sent a signal along a wire that was several miles long.

The inventor who finally succeeded was Samuel Morse of the United States. Morse was an artist, not a scientist, but he had great determination and chose experts for his partners: Leonard Gale, a chemist, and Alfred Vail, an engineer. By 1837, they had a working telegraph. It worked by rapidly opening and closing an electrical circuit to produce signals that sped along a wire. At the other end, the signals were turned into clicking sounds or made marks on paper.

Morse's secret was a **code** of dots and dashes that still bears his name. In 1844, he tapped out the words "What hath God wrought," and the message flashed instantly from Washington, D.C., to Baltimore, Maryland—a distance of 45 miles (65 kilometers).

These cables are being packed ready for the second attempt at laying a permanent cable across the Atlantic.

Impact of the telegraph

The telegraph had enormous impact. In the United States, its incredible speed put the **Pony Express** out of business practically overnight. Soon it spanned continents, linking the world by wire. The "cable" became the best way to send urgent messages.

Morse code was adopted for worldwide use in 1851. Its most famous signal, SOS—three dots, three dashes, three dots—remained the emergency distress code for ships at sea until replaced by **satellite** communication in 1999.

Samuel Morse (1791–1872)

Samuel Finley Breese Morse was born in Massachusetts in 1791. A graduate of Yale University, he studied art and became a successful portrait painter. He spent ten years tinkering with the electric telegraph, making his own equipment from scraps of wire and cotton thread. When his scientific work was too difficult, he found partners who knew more than he did. He petitioned Congress until it agreed to test his new invention. It was a huge success, though Morse later sold his **patent** rights.

1837	1844	1861	1866	1872	1874
Samuel Morse patents his first telegraph.	The Morse-Vail telegraph is demonstrated for the first time.	The first transcontinental telegraph line opens in the United States.	The first transatlantic telegraph cable is laid.	Joseph Stearns invents the duplex telegraph, which can send two messages simultaneously.	Thomas Edison invents the quadruplex telegraph, which can send four messages at once.

Postal Service, 1840

Letters carried by runners or riders on horseback traveled surprisingly quickly. Riders changing horses at intervals could cover 100 miles (160 kilometers) in a day. Private letter-carrying services began in Europe in about 1300. One of the biggest, in Vienna, Austria, employed 20,000 people as mail carriers.

Letter post

In the 1600s, governments began setting up national mail systems. In 1680, the city of London, England, began a mail system that charged a penny per letter. The receiver paid the charge when the letter arrived. When the system proved profitable, the government took it over.

In 1840, Rowland Hill, a retired British schoolteacher, had a better idea. The sender could buy a fixed-charge stamp before sending the letter. He also suggested that letters should be enclosed in envelopes, not just folded and sealed with a blob of wax. This was the start of the modern mail service.

In a modern post office, machines handle the mail far more often than people do. A human hand, though, still delivers each letter to the mailbox.

Handling the mail

Hill's stamps were a huge success, and soon most countries had them. Millions of letters were sent, along with greeting cards—the first Christmas card appeared in 1843. The new railroads and steamships carried mail swiftly.

Letters and packages were collected and sorted in post offices. For 100 years, the sorting was done mostly by hand. Staff read the addresses on the envelopes and packages and put them into bags. In 1963, the United States Postal Service introduced ZIP (zone improvement plan) **codes,** with numbers that a machine could read. Other countries also began using postal codes to speed up automated mail handling.

The first stamps

Before 1840, mail was stamped with ink to show it was paid for. The first adhesive stamps were issued in Great Britain on May 6, 1840—a one-penny black stamp and a two-penny blue, each bearing the head of Queen Victoria. The United States issued its first stamps on July 1, 1847. By 1860, almost every country had begun using stamps on mail. People also started collecting stamps almost at once. The first stamp catalog for collectors was published in 1861.

The 1840 British one-penny black stamp was the world's first adhesive stamp for letters.

The mail sorter

In a modern sorting office, mail is sorted by size and arranged so that all the envelopes face the same way. The stamps are canceled and postmarked. Machines using an electronic system called optical character recognition (OCR) read the postal code. Another machine marks a **bar code** on the mail, so that a third machine can read the code and sort the letters automatically.

The Delivery Bar Code Sorter Input/Output Sub-System, invented in 1999, does all three jobs. It can read addresses on mail of almost any size, print bar codes, weed out badly written addresses and send them off for deciphering, and sort mail by town and street, ready for the mail carrier to deliver. It can sort 40,000 pieces of mail every hour.

1609	1680	1840	1919	1963	1999
The English government takes control of the country's mail service.	William Dockwra starts a postal service in London, England, charging one cent per letter.	Rowland Hill invents the fixed-charge stamp system.	The first regular international mail route is set up, from London to Paris.	The first ZIP codes are used in the United States.	The first fully automated mail sorter is put into use.

Fax Machine, 1843

Fax is short for facsimile, or "copy." A fax machine is used to send documents and pictures along a telephone wire as a series of **coded** electrical pulses. Using a fax machine, people can exchange documents around the world in minutes.

Early experiments

The idea for a copy-sending machine dates from 1843. In that year, a Scot named Alexander Bain **patented** a machine that used a swinging pendulum to trace an image or write a message on paper. The message was sent by electrical impulses and re-created by a second "receiving" pendulum. Bain hoped to use the telegraph as a means of sending pictures, but he never actually sent a fax message.

Attempts at telegraph-faxing

In 1851, another British inventor, Frederick Blakewell, demonstrated a fax machine that was similar to Bain's but had cylinders. It was one of the most talked-about exhibits at the world's fair held that year in London. The French set up the world's first fax line for letters in 1865, using a remarkable machine developed by an Italian inventor named Giovanni Caselli. The Caselli fax was also tried in Britain between London and Manchester.

This brilliant invention was then forgotten, losing out to the telegraph. Governments and businesses were spending money on telegraph links for sending Morse code. They were not interested in the fax system, even though it was potentially more useful.

Arthur Korn of Germany posed in 1906 with the fax machine he invented to send photographs by wire.

Pictures by wire

The invention of the telephone brought a huge expansion in the number of wires linking towns and cities. Long-distance phone calls were being made by the early 1900s, and in 1902 a German scientist named Arthur Korn invented photoelectric **scanning,** a fax system for sending photographs by wire. Korn's invention was taken up quickly by German newspapers. By the 1930s, newspapers across the United States were using a fax system developed by the American Telephone and Telegraph Company to send and receive news photos by wire.

Two problems with early faxes were fuzzy pictures and slow speed. All the data making up a photograph (consisting of black and white dots) had to be scanned, stored, and transmitted using **analog technology.** It could take more than seven minutes to fax one photo.

A modern fax-phone can send a picture or letter in seconds to another machine anywhere in the world.

Speeding up

Digital machines, which store signals in numerical or **binary** code, were developed in the 1960s. By the 1980s, they were proving invaluable to businesses for sending letters, pictures, and technical details across thousands of miles more or less instantaneously.

Using computer technology, electronic digital faxes code the scanned image into binary digits (bits) and transmit them through a **modem.** The scanner moves over the page, measuring the brightness of the spots line by line. This data is compressed, or made smaller, transmitted through a phone line, and then "unsqueezed" to print out a copy of the original image on paper. Modern machines can fax a page in less than ten seconds.

1843	**1902**	**1922**	**1930s**	**1980s**
Alexander Bain patents the first fax machine.	A photo-fax system is invented by Arthur Korn of Germany.	The first images are faxed across the Atlantic by **radio.**	Facsimile telegraph (telephoto) machines are used to send news photographs.	Faster digital fax machines replace analog machines.

Typewriter, 1868

The typewriter became useful when the pace of business life increased so much that people's handwriting could no longer keep up. We can still see the typewriter's legacy in front of us—on our computer keyboards.

The writing machine

In 1714, an Englishman named Henry Mills invented a writing machine, but he found to his dismay that no one wanted him to build it. Writing by hand was quite fast enough. Governments employed clerks to write letters and make copies in neat **longhand.** If they were really busy, clerks used **shorthand** for taking down quick notes and wrote them up later. Until the 1870s, every business had rooms full of clerks writing at desks. Most of them were men.

This early typewriter has the key arrangement that is still in use—look at the top line of black keys. The carriage moved the paper so each key hit a fresh space.

The first typewriter

In the 1800s, inventors wondered if blind people could use a machine to tap out words. Printers were experimenting with machines for setting **type.** The idea was to use keys like those of a piano to move wires up and down. The wires would print letters on paper that could be moved sideways by a carriage device. Christopher Latham Sholes, an American journalist, built a machine with the help of Carlos Glidden and Samuel W. Soulé and **patented** it in 1868. Unfortunately, the keys kept jamming.

The QWERTY keyboard

Sholes got some fresh ideas after reading about another typewriter designed in Britain. By 1870, he had rearranged the letters into the order that is still used today. It is often called QWERTY, after the beginning of the top row of keys. Letters that are commonly used in English were spaced farther apart, so the keys were less likely to jam.

Typewriters take over

The new machine was a hit. Sholes proved it could out-type rival machines. Soon, typewriters were being installed in offices in the United States and Europe. They were easy to use. The ink was on a ribbon that could be quickly changed, and the ability to make lots of copies using **carbon** paper was also useful. Companies hired men—and increasingly, women—to work as typists. This was one of the least expected effects of Sholes's invention—it created new jobs for women.

"Golf ball" typewriters, ideal for home use, were lighter to move around than most office machines.

For a hundred years, the typewriter ruled supreme. In the 1920s, office typing was made easier and faster by James Smathers's electric typewriter, which had an electric motor to drive the touch-sensitive keys. The electric typewriter never completely replaced the manual machine, though. By the 1960s, manufacturers were trying new and faster printing systems such as the "golf ball," a sphere containing letters that moved while the typewriter carriage stayed still.

But the typewriter's day was coming to an end. In the 1980s, along came the PC (personal computer) and the word processor. Very quickly, typewriters became antiques, though some people still use them. A manual typewriter goes on working even in a power outage!

1841	1868	1889	1920s	1960s	1980s
The inked ribbon is invented by Alexander Bain.	Christopher Sholes's typewriter is patented in the United States.	The first portable typewriter, the American Blick, is invented.	The first electric typewriters are used.	The "golf ball" typewriter and the first electronic typewriter, from IBM, are introduced.	Word processors begin to replace typewriters.

Telephone, 1876

By 1860, the telephone seemed an obvious next step after the telegraph. If electrical pulses through a wire could make clicks, then surely they could reproduce the human voice. Telegraphs could send signals but not speech.

The sound problem

There were big problems to overcome. The many sounds of human speech had to be "captured," **coded** electrically, and then decoded so someone at the other end of a wire could hear and understand them.

What was needed was a **microphone** and a receiver. Sound waves in the air would make a thin plate, or **diaphragm,** move or vibrate. This movement could be turned into electrical pulses and sent through a wire. Then, using a second diaphragm to "echo" the vibrations, the pulses would be turned back into sounds. In the 1860s, one inventor tried using sausage skins as diaphragms but quickly gave up!

Here, Alexander Graham Bell is speaking into the mouthpiece of his first telephone (1876). It could both send and receive voice signals.

The first phone call

A teacher, Alexander Graham Bell, cracked the problem in 1875. Bell worked at a school for the deaf in Boston, Massachusetts. He was trying to use the harmonic telegraph—a telegraph with vibrating reeds—to help deaf people hear.

As happens so often in the story of inventions, an accident led the way to success. Bell and his technical assistant, Thomas Watson, were working in adjoining rooms, linked by wires. Watson pulled a reed free from his machine, and as it broke, Bell heard the "snap" through his receiver. This accident spurred them on to build their first telephone.

The great day came in March 1876. Bell was in his laboratory, nervously waiting to test the telephone. In his anxiety, he spilled some acid and called out, "Mr. Watson, come here. I want you!" Watson came running from the next room. He had heard every word clearly over the wire.

The phone catches on

Bell only narrowly beat a rival inventor, Elisha Gray, in **patenting** the telephone. Thus it was Bell who became famous as "the telephone man." He demonstrated his phone on both sides of the Atlantic Ocean. By 1880, there were more than 30,000 phones in use. Dial phones appeared in 1896, so people could now call a local number directly.

Americans were the most enthusiastic phone users. Long-distance lines crossed the continent—and people's voices were still loud and clear, thanks to new booster relays. By 1910, there were seven million phones in the United States, even installed in stores and in street booths.

The telephone transformed world communications. You can now call a friend directly almost anywhere in the world— your voice travels through **fiber-optic cables** and bounces off **satellites.**

Alexander Graham Bell (1847–1922)

Bell was born in Scotland but moved to the United States and taught deaf people. After successfully demonstrating his telephone in 1876, he set up the Bell Telephone Company. In 1878, an improved microphone invented by Thomas Alva Edison made the Bell phone even better. Bell later improved Edison's phonograph, the first sound recording machine. He died in 1922.

Telephones like this began to appear in people's homes in the 1930s. The caller dialed a number using the finger holes.

1876	1891	1900	1956	1965	1988
Alexander Graham Bell invents the telephone.	Almon Strowger patents the automatic exchange.	The first long-distance calls are placed.	The first transatlantic telephone cable is laid.	The first satellite phone calls are made.	The first undersea fiber-optic cables are laid.

Fountain Pen, 1884

The tools we use to write have changed a lot over the years, especially since the invention of ink. Ink was first used in China and Egypt about 2500 B.C.E. People made ink by mixing soot from oil lamps with sticky plant gums. The Egyptians used reed pens. The Greeks and Romans liked metal styluses for writing in clay or wax, but they also used ink pens with split-end nibs. In the Middle Ages in Europe, goose feathers were used to make quill pens, and people carried penknives to sharpen the nibs. Quill pens were used until the 1800s.

Inky fingers

A quill pen had to be dipped into an ink pot every few words. So did the cheap wooden pens used by schoolchildren in the nineteenth century. Inky fingers were a common problem! But what if a pen had its own ink pot? Various inventors tried to make an ink-filled pen, but none of them worked well. Either the ink was too thin and the pen spurted out a "fountain" of ink, or it was too thick, and the pen refused to write at all.

This close-up of a fountain pen writing shows how ink flows down the split in the nib.

Mr. Waterman's pen

The first really good fountain pen was made in 1884 by an insurance salesman named Lewis E. Waterman. He had tried various "improved" ink-filled pens, but they leaked, spoiling his forms and his shirt cuffs. So he designed his own pen, filling it with ink from an eye-dropper bottle.

Later fountain pens had a rubber sac inside for the ink and were filled by a lever that transferred ink from a bottle into the sac. The fountain pen looked sophisticated, so people wanted to own one. It was also convenient—you could carry it around and write letters, sign checks, or fill in forms wherever you were.

Cartridges, balls, and other tips

Most modern pens have ink-filled, drop-in cartridges. Other pens, such as the ballpoint, the felt-tip, and the fiber-tip, also have their own ink supplies. However, their writing points are designed differently.

The modern ballpoint pen appeared in 1938. Invented by Hungarian brothers Laszlo and Georg Biró, the ballpoint used thick printing ink that dried almost immediately. This meant that the ink did not smudge. Many people liked the smooth ball action, and they quickly became popular. In some countries they are still known as "biros."

The felt-tip pen is a modern version of the ancient reed pen. It appeared in the 1960s.

1884	1904	1927	1938	1953	1963
Lewis Waterman designs his fountain pen.	George Parker of the United States invents the lever-fill for pens.	The ink cartridge is invented.	The Biró brothers make their first ballpoint pen.	Mass-produced ballpoints go on sale in France.	The felt-tipped pen is invented in Japan.

Photocopier, 1938

If a person living in 1800 wanted to send the same letter to ten people, the only way was to copy it ten times. Copying was slow and boring work. It kept thousands of workers occupied.

Carbon copies

Early in the nineteenth century, a faster method was invented, using ink-soaked **carbon** paper. A clerk slipped a sheet of carbon paper between two sheets of writing paper, wrote on the top sheet—and there was a "carbon copy" on the bottom sheet. Carbon paper became really useful when offices began using typewriters in the 1870s. A typist could make several copies at once, using several sheets of carbon paper placed between plain sheets.

Duplication

In 1888, a machine called the duplicator was invented to make multiple copies from an original document. It was made in London by Hungarian David Gestetner, who used a typewriter to punch holes in a waxed-fiber sheet in order to produce a stencil. The stencil was inked, and a paper-covered roller pushed over it to print each copy. The Roneo machine of 1900, invented by a Czech named A. D. Klaber, was faster because it used a roller-drum, turned by a handle. It could produce 5,000 copies from one original. A new and useful accessory to deal with the mounting piles of paper copies was the paper clip, which was invented in about 1900!

How the photocopier was invented

Carbon paper was fine for copying letters as you typed. But how could you copy an old letter? Photographing it was messy and too expensive for office or school. During the 1930s, a young physicist named Chester Carlson was working in a **patent** office. He spent his spare time trying to invent a clean, fast "photocopying" machine to copy patent drawings. Rather than using chemicals or photographs, he experimented with xerography, or "dry copying." This process uses electrical charges, light, and heat to transfer images from one sheet of paper to another.

How a photocopier works

A light system with a lamp, lens, and mirrors projects an image of the document onto a metal drum that carries a negative electrical charge. The light removes the charge from all but the dark areas of the image—these keep their negative charge. Particles of **toner** with a positive charge are put on the drum and stick to the dark areas of the image, because positive and negative charges attract each other. The copy of the image is transferred onto paper and fixed by heat before it comes out of the machine.

Slow success

Carlson succeeded in 1938. He reproduced on paper a copy of a handwritten date and a place name: "10–22–38 Astoria." His basic equipment included a glass slide, a light bulb, a light-sensitive metal plate, and some moss spores—his version of toner—that stuck to the image. World War II began in 1939, and Carlson did not get very far with his photocopier until 1947, when the Haloid Company—later the Xerox Corporation—took up the idea.

Chester Carlson (1906–68) was turned down many times before he found a company to sell his new photocopier.

The first office copiers were expensive and needed special paper. Copiers did not become common until the 1960s, when plain paper copiers went on sale. Carlson, however, did well from selling his invention and unlike many other inventors, he became a millionaire.

1888	1938	1947	1958	1960s	1970s
The first stencil-duplicating machine is invented by David Gestetner.	Chester Carlson makes his first successful test copy.	The Haloid Company (later Xerox) buys the rights to xerography.	The first Xerox office copiers go on sale.	The first plain paper copiers are introduced.	Color copiers come into use.

Communications Satellite, 1960

In 1945, writer Arthur C. Clarke made what seemed like a crazy prediction. He said that in a few years, **satellites** orbiting Earth would provide world coverage for telephone calls and television. However, no satellite had yet been launched into space. Even in 1956, leading astronomers were still saying space travel just would not happen.

Satellites go into space

Telstar (1962) relayed TV pictures across the Atlantic Ocean. The satellite was followed by Telstar 2 in 1963.

In 1957, the Russians launched *Sputnik I,* the first satellite to orbit Earth. Soon Clarke was proved right. He had written about satellites in **geosynchronous orbit**—positioned above the equator at a height of more than 22,000 miles (35,400 kilometers), orbiting in time with Earth and so maintaining the same position over the surface. Such a satellite is a fixed target for signals from the ground, relaying them back across oceans and continents.

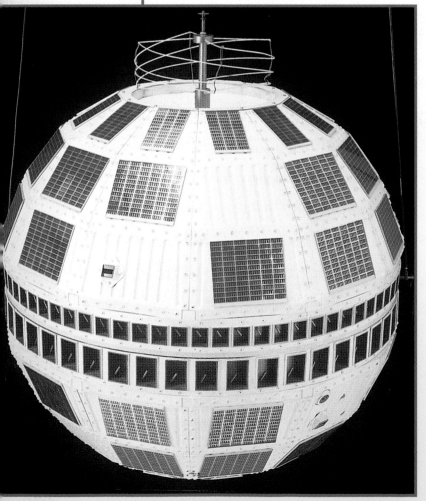

First comsats

The United States launched the first communications satellite, or "comsat," in 1960. Called *Echo I,* it was a shiny balloon 33 yards (30 meters) around. Crude though it was, *Echo I* proved that it was possible to bounce **radio** and television signals off a satellite in space and back to the ground.

In July 1962, a much better comsat called *Telstar* was launched. For the first time, television viewers in the United States could watch live pictures from Europe. *Telstar* became so famous that a pop song was written in its honor. It could handle just one TV transmission and 60 phone calls at a time.

Entertainment and education

Communications satellites were successful because people wanted to see live events, such as the Olympic Games. India and other developing countries used satellite TV to educate people who lived in remote regions without schools and colleges.

Satellites are expensive to build and launch, but television and telephone companies are willing to pay a lot of money for satellite time. Some companies started their own satellite broadcasting channels and beamed programs around the world into the homes of people with small dish **antennae.**

Today, a ring of satellites orbits Earth, each one relaying TV channels and phone calls from transmitters to receivers.

Satellite power

Satellite TV broadcasters now rival ground-based stations. Satellite power has grown tremendously. By the 1980s, Earth was ringed by Intelsat communications satellites, each able to relay 33,000 telephone calls and as many as 60 television channels at the same time. There seems to be no limit to the satellites' power.

1957	1960	1962	1965	1980s	1990s
The first satellite to orbit Earth is launched.	*Echo I* proves that satellites work.	*Telstar* beams live pictures across the Atlantic Ocean.	The "Early Bird" is the world's first commercial communications satellite.	Intelsat satellites boost communications capacity.	Satellite broadcasting is in worldwide use.

Mobile Phone, 1979

Until the 1920s, all telephones relied on wires to carry voice signals as electrical impulses. There was also a "wireless" way to transmit sounds—**radio.** From that developed something seen everywhere today, the mobile phone.

Radio phones

The first phones without wires were radio phones. These sent signals through the air as radio waves. Reginald Fessenden spoke the first words "on the air" in 1900 in the United States, though his signal traveled less than a mile (1.6 kilometers). By 1906, he was playing the violin over the airwaves! As shortwave radio **technology** improved, the Detroit police tried portable radio phones in 1921. Car phones became popular with highway patrols in a number of countries.

In 1946, a mobile phone service was tried in St. Louis, Missouri. In 1947, Bell Laboratories came up with the idea of using transmitter "cells" to pass on phone messages from one mobile phone to the next. The cell phone sends and receives radio signals to and from transmitters arranged in areas called cells. The **antenna-**transmitter in the nearest cell picks up the call and passes it on to the next cell, and into the main telephone network. Without modern electronics, the early experiments were not very effective, since only one person could speak at a time.

The changing phone

By the 1960s, many people had more than one phone at home, but almost all phones were plugged in. There were cordless phones, but callers could not wander far from the base unit that was wired into the phone line. People wanted phones that they could take anywhere. These were made possible by rapid changes in **telecommunications.**

The first automatic telephone exchange was opened in Nebraska in 1921. It was mechanical and relied on **analog** technology. The world's first electronic phone exchange began working in New Jersey in 1965. Computerized **digital** technology, with information being represented by electrical pulses, made the telephone system faster and more efficient, and it turned the cell phone into a truly mobile personal communications device.

The cell phone reappears

Bell's electronic cell phone system was finally tested in Chicago in 1978. In 1979, the Ericsson Company of Sweden demonstrated their new cell phone, and within two years there was a mobile phone network across Scandinavia. Soon, mobile phones could be seen on city streets everywhere as cell networks were set up.

It was easy to listen in on the early phones that used analog signals. Modern digital phones are much more secure from eavesdroppers. Analog signals are changed into digital **binary code,** giving clearer transmission. The code is then changed back into analog signals so the sounds can be heard. Phones with **microchips** can also store numbers and access information.

Mobile phones in a range of models, old and new, are used for everything from "I missed the bus" calls to big business deals.

The global phone network

In the 1990s, mobile phones became a common sight all over the world and were especially popular with young people. In 1999, the first new "media phones" came on the market, based on WAP (Wireless Applications Protocol). With a media phone, a person can not only talk to other phone users, but also access the **Internet** and send and receive e-mail.

1938	1947	1970	1979	1983	1999
Al Gross of the United States invents a "walkie talkie."	Bell Laboratories introduces a "cell" linking system.	Direct dialing is available between New York City and London.	The Ericsson mobile phone is launched in Sweden.	The first commercial cell phone system is set up in the United States.	WAP phones extend the range of phone services by offering Internet access.

E-mail, 1982

There are all kinds of ways to send messages—by letter, by telegraph, by telephone, and by fax. The newest, and the one that has grown most rapidly, is e-mail.

How e-mail began

E-mail grew in the 1980s as a by-product of the **Internet.** The Internet grew from a network of computers, linked so that information could be exchanged between them.

At first, the Internet was used only by computer experts in universities and government offices, but starting in 1991, commercial companies began to offer Internet access to anyone with a computer, a **modem,** and a phone connection. The modem was a 1950s invention that found its place in **telecommunications** in the 1980s. It connects a computer to the phone lines, allowing it to exchange information with other computers.

The growth of e-mail

By the 1980s, many millions of people all over the world had phones in their homes, and millions were also buying cheap PCs for home use. Schools, too, were going online to use this new source of information and exchange. Everything was in place for another communications revolution.

A popular use for the new computer network was to send messages as electronic mail, or e-mail. Often, teenagers were the first to have fun with this new **technology.** They began sending messages to each other. Businesses soon realized the importance of this new super-fast communications system.

Using e-mail

Anyone with an Internet connection can get his or her own e-mail address from an Internet service provider (ISP). The provider acts as a collector for all mail and sends it to the right address. To send an e-mail, you open a mail program on your computer and type a message with the correct e-mail address of the person or persons it is going to. An e-mail can include attached files such as documents or pictures.

An e-mail is a sequence of signals. The data in the file you created is transmitted **digitally** through the phone system by a modem. This changes computer data into electrical signals that can travel along metal wires or **fiber-optic cables,** or through the air as **radio** waves. The e-mail is collected by the ISP. When the receiver wants to read his e-mail, he accesses the ISP through the Internet and opens his mail program. Incoming mail appears in the inbox and can be read on screen, saved, or printed out.

You may receive e-mails that you do not want. There is junk e-mail just as there is junk mail. But e-mail is very useful to people who need to exchange information quickly. People working from home, for example, can send letters or even whole books at the click of a button.

People can access the Internet from any computer linked to the phone network. E-mails have become part of business, school, and home life for many computer users.

1958	1982	1980s	1989	1991	1990s
The modem is invented.	Western Union starts Easylink e-mail service in the United States.	More people buy PCs for home and school use.	The World Wide Web (WWW) on the Internet is created.	Private companies start offering Internet connections.	E-mail systems expand rapidly in many countries.

Timeline

Prehistoric times	Sticks of charcoal, or burned wood, are used for drawing.
3500 B.C.E.	Cuneiform writing is invented in Sumeria.
3000 B.C.E.	**Hieroglyphic** writing is developed in Egypt.
2500 B.C.E.	The first Egyptian **scroll-**books are produced.
2500 B.C.E.	The oldest known map is made in Babylon.
600 B.C.E.	The Roman alphabet is introduced.
105 C.E.	The first paper is made in China.
350	The oldest known codex is printed.
868	The first book, the Chinese *Diamond Sutra,* is printed.
1200	The first books are made with paper. They are still handwritten.
1454–45	The first book (the Bible) is printed by Johannes Gutenberg on a press using movable **type.**
1565	The first written description of a pencil is recorded.
1570	The first atlas, or book of maps, is published.
1794	Claude Chappé invents semaphore.
1796	The process of lithography is invented.
1811	Koenig and Bauer produce the first steam printing press.
1829	The first braille book is produced by Louis Braille.
1837	Samuel Morse **patents** his first telegraph.
1840	Englishman Rowland Hill invents the fixed-charge postage stamp.
1843	Alexander Bain patents the first fax machine.
1844	The Morse-Vail telegraph is first demonstrated.
	Richard Hoe invents the rotary printing press.
1868	Christopher Latham Sholes patents the first typewriter.

1876	Alexander Graham Bell invents the telephone.
1884	Lewis Waterman designs the first fountain pen.
1888	David Gestetner invents the first stencil-duplicating machine.
1895	The first mechanical pencils are produced.
1900	The first long-distance telephone calls are placed.
1902	Arthur Korn of Germany invents a photo-fax system.
1920s	The first electric typewriters are produced.
1922	The first images are faxed across the Atlantic Ocean by **radio.**
1938	The Biró brothers make the first ballpoint pen.
	Chester Carlson produces the first successful photocopier.
1955	The first "talking books" are produced.
1957	*Sputnik I,* the first **satellite** to orbit Earth, is launched.
1958	The **modem** is invented.
1960s	Computerized phototypesetting begins.
1960	*Echo I,* the first communications satellite, is launched.
1962	*Telstar* beams live pictures across the Atlantic Ocean.
1963	ZIP codes are introduced in the United States.
1965	The first satellite phone calls are made.
1970s	Color photocopiers first come into use.
1979	The Ericsson mobile phone is launched in Sweden.
1980s	Computerized **digital typesetting** and page make-up revolutionize printing.
1982	Western Union starts its Easylink e-mail service in the U.S.
1991	Firms start offering **Internet** access to the public.
1999	Fully automated mail sorting machines are used.

Glossary

analog representation of numerical or physical quantities by physical variables, such as electrical voltage changes

antenna device for collecting electrical and radio signals in the atmosphere

bar code striped marking with coded information that can be read electronically when a laser scans it

binary information storage system using only the digits 0 and 1

Buddhist follower of the teachings of the Buddha, Siddhartha Gautama, who lived in India from about 563 to 483 B.C.E.

carbon natural substance that takes several forms, including charcoal, soot, diamonds, and coal

code system of symbols or signs used for storing and sending information. A code may be secret or made for a machine to understand.

diaphragm thin disc that vibrates in response to sound waves

digital form of recording data in which sound or pictures are represented by binary numbers

electric current flow of electricity through a metal wire

electromagnetism force produced when an electric current flows through a coil of wire

fiber-optic cable thin glass or plastic tubes bundled together as a means of communication that can send light signals very fast

geometry branch of mathematics dealing with measuring and comparing lines, angles, and figures

geosynchronous orbit placement of a satellite in space at such a height and speed that it stays in position above the same point on Earth's surface

hieroglyphics picture-writing used in ancient Egypt and the Americas in which a symbol stood for a word, a sound, or an idea

Internet network of computers that are linked so that they can exchange information

latitude distance of a place (in degrees) north or south of the equator

longhand writing by hand with a pen or pencil

longitude distance of a place (in degrees) east or west of the prime meridian, a line that runs through Greenwich, England, linking the North and South Poles

magnetic field lines of force around the poles of a magnet, which are seen when iron filings are scattered around a magnet

microchip tiny electronic device with circuits built up on a wafer of silicon

modem device that links a computer to the telephone system, allowing computers to communicate with one another through the Internet

patent official document confirming ownership of a particular invention or process

Pony Express mail service set up in the United States in 1860 using riders on fast horses

printing plate metal plate carrying a photographically imposed image of letters and pictures; the part of a printing press that transfers the ink onto the paper either directly or indirectly

radio sending sounds through the air without wires

Renaissance period in European history (roughly 1350 to 1550) noted for new ideas in art and science and the rediscovery of ancient learning

satellite small planet or spacecraft in orbit around a larger body

scan to look at every part of something. An electronic scanner sweeps a beam across a surface to pick up any data it can read.

scroll book written on a long piece of paper rolled on two sticks and unrolled to read

shorthand system of fast writing using symbols and shortened forms of words

sign mark, picture, or other symbol that gives information

technology applying of scientific knowledge in practical ways, using methods and machines made by inventors to make people's lives better

telecommunications all the means of sending messages over long distances electronically, such as by telephone, radio, and the Internet

toner type of dry ink used in a photocopier

type letters, numbers, and other characters used in printing

typesetting arranging letters to make words that can then be printed

More Books to Read

Erlbach, Arlene. *The Kids' Invention Book.* Minneapolis: The Lerner Publishing Group, 1998.

Parker, Janice. *Messengers, Morse Code & Modems: The Science of Communication.* Austin, Tex.: Raintree Steck-Vaughn, 2000.

Parker, Steve. *Communications.* Parsippany, N.J.: Silver Burdett Press, 1998.

Tesar, Jenny E., and Bryan H. Bunch. *The Blackbirch Encyclopedia of Science & Invention.* Woodbridge, Conn.: The Blackbirch Press, 2001.

Index

alphabets 7, 14

ballpoint pen 35
bar code 27
beacon 18
Bell, Alexander Graham
    32–33
body language 4
books 5, 11, 12–13, 14,
    15, 16, 22, 23
braille 22–23
Braille, Louis 22–23

carbon copies 31, 36
cell phone 40–41
Chappé, Claude 18, 19
clay and wax tablets 6, 7,
    8, 10
codes 4, 18, 22, 24, 25,
    26, 28, 29, 32, 41
codex 12
communications
    revolution 5, 42
computers 5, 21, 42, 43
cuneiform writing 7

digital technology 21, 29,
    40–41, 43
duplicator 36

electromagnetism 24
e-mail 5, 39, 42–43

fax machine 5, 28–29
fiber-optic cables 33, 43

flag signaling 18, 19
fountain pen 34–35

graphite 16, 17
Gutenberg, Johannes 14,
    15

hieroglyphics 4, 7

Internet 41, 42–43

lithography 21

mail sorting 26–27
maps 8–9
media phone 41
Mercator, Gerardus 9
mobile phone 40–41
Morse code 24, 25, 28
Morse, Samuel 24, 25

optical scanners 23, 27

paper 10–11, 20
paperbacks 13
papyrus 10, 12, 16
parchment 10, 12
PC (personal computer)
    31, 42
pencil 16–17
photocopier 36–37
pigeon post 18
Pony Express 25
postal service 26–27
postal code 26, 27

printing 5, 12, 13,
    14–15, 20–21

quill pen 16, 34
QWERTY keyboard 30

radio 29, 38, 43
radio phone 40
Renaissance 15
Roneo machine 36
Rosetta Stone 4

satellites 5, 9, 25, 33,
    38–39
scanning 23, 29
scribes 6, 10
scrolls 12
semaphore 18–19
shorthand 30
signatures 7
stamps 26, 27
Sumerian writing 6–7

"talking books" 23
telegraph 19, 24–25, 28,
    32
telephone 28–29, 32–33,
    38, 39, 40–41
typesetting 14, 15,
    20–21
typewriter 5, 30–31, 36

word processor 31
writing 5, 6–7, 16, 30